ONCE UPON A WAR

GROWING UP IN THE LONDON BLITZ

Beryl MacDonald

Otek Press   Salem, Oregon

© 2007 by Beryl MacDonald

ISBN(10 digit): 0-9791954-0-3
ISBN(13 digit): 978-0-9791954-0-2

Library of Congress Control Number: 2006940855

Layout & design by DIMI PRESS

Cover by Dick Lutz

PREFACE

This is a true story but to protect the privacy of people mentioned I have changed all of the surnames and many of the first names. All of the events really happened and all of the people were real people.

When war broke out in 1939 I was eleven years old. When war ended in 1945 I was 17, and ten months later I arrived in the United States as a war bride. I was eighteen. This is my story of those years, of growing up during wartime.

I never kept a diary, except in my brain, but I remembered it all: the people and places, the sights and sounds, the smells and tastes, the hot, the cold, the happy, the sad. It's all still there.

This is the way I remember it.

Children waiting for war

Betty   *   Michael   *   Beryl

CHAPTER 1

ONCE UPON A TIME THERE WAS A WAR ..

… but in that 1939 summer there was no war yet, only the reminders of what was to come. Otherwise, life in my London suburb was the same as I always remembered it.

I was eleven years old, a small schoolgirl, but it was vacation time and we spent our days playing in the park and swimming in the pool. Small boys sailed their toy boats on the pond, sharing the water with long-necked white-backed swans, while bigger boys played cricket.

Streets lined with red brick houses were quiet except for the occasional jingling bell of the ice cream man, but the busy High Road was a roar of big red buses, taxis, cars and lorries, with shoppers crowding the sidewalks. The Salvation Army band played outside the White Horse pub, tambourines and trumpets blending with the laughter and tinkle of glasses that filtered through the half-open door.

Suddenly, the air raid siren on the police station roof wailed to a crescendo, and the sounds of buses, bells, taxis and tambourines were engulfed. Then the wailing fell away and the London noise returned. It was only a test.

Shop windows displayed the bounty of the British Empire. Chocolates and cheeses, bananas and beef, silk, satin, tobacco and toys. On the news racks the Daily Express vied for attention with the Telegraph and Daily Mail: pictures of duchesses at a garden party and boats at the Henley Regatta; advertisements for furs, and for Cooks' Tours of the Continent. But there was other news as well: Anti-aircraft units in training; what to do in case of an air raid.

Men tended roses in their gardens while their wives sewed blackout curtains from heavy dark fabric. Between our games, we children talked about evacuation. If war came we were going to the country. It would be an adventure, like going away to camp, and we looked forward to living in thatched roof cottages, or even in a castle with turrets and a drawbridge!

August arrived. The first Monday was a national holiday, and the carnival came to Hampstead Heath for the long weekend. Calliope sounds, petrol smells, coconut shies and shooting galleries; swings, roundabouts and bumper cars; and giant pink puffs of candy floss. The high diver plunged from his lofty perch into a flaming tank, drowning the fire in a gigantic splash, while spectators clutched their prizes of cheap Japanese china. But from the noisy crowd came fragments of conversation in strange languages. Hungarian? Czech? Polish? French? Dutch? Danish? I didn't understand any of it, but people talked about the refugees beginning to arrive.

In late August we went back to school but not to lessons. We carried gas masks, and backpacks that contained clothes and underwear, pajamas, socks, towel and toothbrush. And a bag of sandwiches and fruit - this might be the day we did not get home for tea.

We learned how to put on and adjust our gas masks, how to test for leaks by placing a piece of paper over the filter and breathing in. If the paper fell off the straps were too loose. Our gray rubber masks had metal "snouts" but small children had brightly colored ones which they called "Mickey Mouse" masks. Babies had large contraptions that had to be pumped by hand.

Each day we went through the routine of following the teachers out to the buses that would take us to the station, but the buses were not there - it was only practice. And then September came; Hitler was in Poland, and the buses were lined up along the curb.

CHAPTER 2

THE BIG EVACUATION

The station was noisy and smoky-smelling and the black steam engine roared and hissed. Behind a barrier a crowd had gathered, mostly women, waving and calling out as we climbed on board, but when the train lurched out of the station the crowd of mothers disappeared from view.

London buildings gave way to hedgerows and green fields where horses, cows and sheep grazed. I loved riding on a train but sometimes the train stopped on a dismal siding. What were we waiting for? A troop train? Munitions? Another evacuee train? Then we were off again, to more fields and villages. We ate our soggy sandwiches and fruit, and got hungry again. At last we saw brick houses, a town, and in late afternoon we stepped on to the platform. We had arrived in Northampton.

Buses took us to a school. More waiting. More buses. I was now in a smaller group of about twenty children and two teachers, and my younger sister and brother, Betty and Michael, were with me. The bus took us to a neighborhood on the edge of town, almost in the country. We began walking up a hill, past houses of brick and stucco with their owners watching from the doorways. No castles with turrets, not even a thatched roof!

The teachers looked over their lists of families that had agreed to take evacuees, and children disappeared into houses, sometimes in pairs. But no-one wanted three! As dusk approached we were the only ones left! We must have seemed a forlorn-looking trio, tired and rumpled, still wearing our backpacks which had seemed to grow heavier during the long day. While the teachers tried to decide the best way to split us up, we heard, "We'll take them," and looked up to see a tall, lanky man running down the street. He and his wife had only signed up for two, but thought they could manage an extra one, at least for a while. So we moved in with the Browns and their little boy.

CHAPTER 3

MY NEW LIFE AS AN EVACUEE

The local schools weren't ready yet, but the teachers gave us no time to be homesick. The days were warm and sunny so they marched us, two by two, into the country, along narrow lanes where elderberries hung in big red clusters. We climbed over stiles and picked blackberries in a field while we warily eyed the horses, cows and sheep. On Sunday we went two by two to church.

Northampton, like many Midland towns, had Market Days. On Wednesdays and Saturdays the central square came to life and people crowded between stalls full of *everything*. Pots and pans and patent leather shoes; green cabbages, red apples and purple cardigans; wicker baskets and Wellington boots; toys, teddy bears, teapots, china cups, and chickens for Sunday dinner. I loved market days. My London neighborhood had no market square, only rows of shops.

Our parents came on the train, bringing suitcases full of clothes and toys and favorite books. My new school uniforms arrived. They didn't fit, but Mrs Brown made some alterations, and at last we were able to start school.

Northampton School for Girls shared its building with the girls' school from Brondesbury where I was a new student; the local girls were there in the mornings, and we had afternoons until 5:30. We had our own teachers, books and uniforms, and our paths seldom crossed, although a few messages chalked on blackboards expressed some rivalry and resentment. They called us cockneys; we called them country bumpkins!

The government issued identity cards and I now had a number as well as a name. I remembered that number for many years, but the proliferation of area codes, zip codes and pin numbers has finally crowded it out of my memory.

November 5th was Guy Fawkes Day. All my life this had been a day for fun. Guy Fawkes had been the leader of the 1605 Gunpowder Plot to blow up the Houses of Parliament and the King. But the plot had been discovered, the traitors had been executed, and Parliament and the King had been saved. For more than three hundred years people had celebrated with bonfires and fireworks, but this year we had no celebration. No bonfires to light the Luftwaffe's way; no rockets or Roman Candles, not even sparklers.

The days grew colder. Northampton is located north of the 52nd parallel, and winter days are short, so when we left school at 5:30 it was completely, totally dark. Because of the blackout there were no street lamps and no lighted windows in houses or shops. The school organized convoys, and all teachers and students who lived in the same part of town left together, dropping out one by one as homes were reached. Except on rare moonlit nights we were a group of disembodied voices. But the convoys were fun!

Three extra children had proved too much for the Browns, so I moved to a new billet with the Johnsons. They had a little boy and Mrs. Johnson's parents lived with them. I called the Johnsons Auntie and Uncle but, to avoid confusion, her parents were Uncle Fred and Auntie Em. Again, I was accepted as part of the family and soon felt at home.

Christmas was coming. Although there were still no air raids in London, the government was encouraging people to leave their children in the country. A few of my friends went home, but I stayed in Northampton and spent my first Christmas away from my family.

Christmas holidays in London had always been filled with activities. At least one of the neighbors gave a party for the children, and there were parties at school and Sunday school, often with presents tied on to the big Christmas tree. My father's club put on a big party, followed by a pantomime. One Christmas I went to a West End theatre to see "Cinderella" with real white ponies pulling the coach across the stage. Another time I was taken to the Bertram Mills Circus. There were clowns and a lion tamer, and koala bears riding bicycles, but my favorites were the trapeze artists.

No pantomimes or circuses this year! But plans were made to keep us from feeling too deprived. There were several parties at school, and excursions to the cinema and repertory theatre, but the highlight was a train trip to Stratford-on-Avon where we toured the Shakespeare houses and the church. The older girls saw a play, but it was too adult for my age group; *our* Shakespeare was carefully edited! We spent the afternoon sliding on the solidly frozen river and having tea in a 16th century Tudor tea room.

Christmas Day was very, very cold, but there were blazing fires in the fireplaces and the dinner and tea tables were laden with wonderful Christmas foods: turkey with stuffing, plum pudding and mince pies, and a giant fruitcake encased in marzipan and white icing. Parcels sent from London had been quickly hidden away so the pillowcase I hung at the end of my bed on Christmas Eve was filled next morning with books, puzzles, tins of toffees, boxes of handkerchiefs, and the Parker fountain pen I had hoped for. A good pen was a status symbol at school, and my old one was from Woolworth's. My new family had even bought me the blue fur-trimmed moccasin slippers I wanted, and there were money orders from assorted aunts and uncles, even one from my former Sunday School teacher. I was an avid letter writer in those days - it paid off!

The snow came, more snow than I had ever seen. Huge flakes whirled out of a lead-gray sky, covering gardens and fields. It lay in ribbons along the tops of fences and clung delicately to tree branches. Even the jagged dry stone walls were smooth under their soft white blanket. My friend Sheila joined me for Wellington-booted hikes. The river had overflowed its banks during the Autumn rains, and the biting cold had turned river and fields into a vast solidly-frozen lake. People skated behind the Vicarage, but Sheila and I had no skates so we walked and slid along the river where summer weeds were eerie green shapes locked into the ice. That winter was the coldest England had had for decades.

In February the Government decreed that clocks were to be moved forward an extra hour because of the blackout. Now we could go home from school in daylight. The days grew longer but the snow lingered, melting slowly into slushy gray piles even as warming sun brought the first green to the trees. As winter floods receded, the field at the end of the lane became a forest of bulrushes, higher than my head, and tiny woolly lambs frolicked among the sheep.

The Easter holidays came and, as at Christmas, the school planned lots of special activities. We hiked to Nobottle Woods and had a picnic lunch under the trees where primroses were a bright yellow carpet. Buses took us to castles and manor houses, and we strolled through the elegant gardens of Compton Wingates, admired the peacocks roaming the grounds at Warwick, and climbed through the ruins of Kenilworth. There was another trip to Stratford-on-Avon which looked so different with the snow and ice gone. There were white swans on the river and green grass along the banks.

On Good Friday I went with Uncle Fred to the market in Banbury. He had a leather goods business and traveled to all the market towns in the area - when he had enough petrol. While he set up his stall and display of dog collars, leashes and soft chamois cloths, I went off across the square to see the famous Banbury Cross, from nursery rhyme days. I was quite disappointed to find only a simple stone Celtic cross instead of the giant crucifix I had always imagined. And not a cockhorse in sight! I listened to a carillon playing "When I Survey The Wondrous Cross" while I ate a Banbury cake, a flat, flaky pastry, bulging with raisins and currants. It was very good, but really no different from the ones they sold in the London bakeries.

The next week Uncle Fred took me to market in Rugby, and on the way we passed the famous school of Tom Brown's Schooldays. One market was much like another, and even the same merchants were there, but Rugby had a slaughterhouse nearby. I strolled past the sheds where men were butchering the animals, staring in fascination at the river of blood running along the gutter. I don't know why I wasn't horrified. Perhaps I saw it as an extension of the butcher shop where we got our Sunday beef to go with the Yorkshire pudding! Back at the stall I shared the lunch hamper with Uncle Fred.

School began again and summer brought rounders games and tennis lessons. I went swimming in the River Nene and sat under great trees where cuckoos, never seen, called softly from dense foliage.

I made friends with some of the local girls. Madge lived in a 400 year old stone house on the edge of the moor and we had great fun exploring along the river. Pat lived on a dairy farm and had her own pony which she sometimes let me ride around the paddock, but I gave the cows a wide berth - I was terrified of their horns! One day, when Pat wasn't home, their housekeeper Joan asked if I would like to help drive the cows down to the pasture. I thought I'd be safe behind the herd (there were about 20), so I rode Pat's bike while Joan walked, tapping an occasional rump to keep them moving. The cows seemed to know where to go, and they sauntered out of the barnyard and along the lanes. When Joan went ahead and opened the gate they trooped obediently into the field, except for one cow who kept right on going down the lane. Joan went after her while I held the big wide gate open, blocking the narrow road. Soon the recalcitrant beast was charging right at me! It might as well have been Tyrranosaurus Rex! I would rather have been in the path of a big double-decker London bus! But just before I died of terror the cow turned into the pasture and went trotting off to join her friends.

Marketplace

Still there after 60 years

CHAPTER 4

FOOD RATIONING

Everyone had a ration book now and basic foods like meat, sugar, tea and butter could not be bought without it. Other foods, including eggs, were scarce, and oranges and bananas were only memories, but we had potatoes every day and there were plenty of dreaded green vegetables and turnips. I was beginning to grow more rapidly and always seemed to be ravenously hungry.

Auntie and Auntie Em cooked together and found many ways to stretch the meat ration. Sunday dinner always began with large portions of Yorkshire Pudding and rich brown gravy. The roast beef was sliced thin and carefully apportioned so there would be enough left for Monday's Shepherd's Pie or Rissoles. A few sausages, which we could watch being made right in the butcher's shop, would be baked in a pudding we called "Toad in the Hole", and it took only a small amount of chopped bacon to make Bacon Roll, a savory steamed pudding, fragrant with onions and parsley. But not all of their culinary efforts met with approval. One day, when that week's meat ration had been totally used up, Auntie Em made a casserole of tripe with onion sauce. I still remember how awful it was, like eating the crepe soles from a pair of shoes! She never cooked it again.

There was always dessert of some sort. Leftover bread went into Bread Pudding or the more elaborate Queen of Puddings, the fruit trees in the back garden yielded apples and plums for cooking in various ways, or we might have simple cooked rice drizzled with milk and sugar.

I loved Sunday high tea. The dining room table was extended and set with the best china. There were platters of thinly sliced buttered bread, jam, tiny salmon paste sandwiches, and bowls of peaches, Blancmange, or Trifle. In summer there was watercress and just-picked tomatoes and lettuce from Uncle Fred's big back garden. Always there was cake, homemade or from the baker: Victoria Sandwich or Butterfly cakes or Madeleines.

CHAPTER 5

THE WAR COMES CLOSER

At Dunkirk an amazing armada of fishing boats and tiny cruisers helped to rescue the British army from the beaches. The Germans were only eighteen miles from England now, but RAF pilots in their marvelous Spitfires zoomed out over the English Channel, and the Luftwaffe soon gave up. We called it the Battle of Britain, and Prime Minister Churchill, in his famous speech, acclaimed the "few" to whom we owed so much, while he exhorted and encouraged the rest of us.

France surrendered and Mademoiselle came to French class looking sad. Her family was still there. We were soon singing a new song, "The last time I saw Paris, her heart was warm and gay…"

England prepared to be invaded. Signposts disappeared from the lanes, and church bells were not to ring except to signal an invasion, but the countryside looked as peaceful as ever, and there was still no bombing in London. So, at last, I was to go home for the summer holiday.

CHAPTER 6

LONDON VACATION

My London neighborhood looked the same but I felt strangely out of place after almost a year away. Part of our small back garden was now occupied by an Anderson air raid shelter. It was constructed of sections of corrugated steel, half below ground, half above, with earth mounded over the top. Ours was painted green and the top was a riot of brightly colored summer flowers. Steps led down to a little green door, and the inside was cool with wooden bunks, rugs and cushions. A perfect playhouse, or a fort for my brother. We sometimes had our tea in there.

Walking home through the park, after swimming, I heard the air raid warning. Children jumped from swings and seesaws, women with babies in prams ran from the rose garden, and everyone rushed to the shelters. We crowded into a windowless brick building as the siren died away, and waited for the air raid to begin; but it was quiet outside and after a while we heard the All Clear.

One morning, while riding my bicycle, I saw people clustered around a gap in a high wooden fence so I squeezed through to see what everyone was staring at. Out in the field a barrage balloon twisted and turned and pulled against its moorings, shimmering in the sun like a great silver monster. The balloons looked very small up in the sky, and this was the first time I had seen one up close. I knew I absolutely must have a photograph to take back to Northampton, so I pedaled home, grabbed my small box camera and pedaled back, hoping the balloon would still be down. It was!

I peered into the viewfinder and clicked the shutter. Suddenly, RAF men were running across the field towards me, and I looked up to see two very, very tall policemen. I explained that I just wanted a picture to show my friends, but they took my camera and bundled me into a nearby police car. My shocked mother opened the door, but after she had assured them that we were all British subjects I was set free. I got my camera back next day at the police station, but the film was gone.

I decided to devote the rest of my summer holiday to safer pursuits. The art teachers at school had announced a competition for a drawing or painting, with prizes. Each day I sat outside with pencils and watercolors making a painting of our Anderson shelter. I was pleased with my picture and put it into my suitcase. In August I took the train back to Northampton.

Classes began and we were reminded that there was still a week before the deadline for the Art competition. I looked for my painting but it was nowhere to be found. If I wanted to enter I would have to do another picture. Every day I sat by my bedroom window sketching the little stone church that was just across the field behind the house. The drawing was good and I managed with my watercolors to capture the brown and beige tones of the ancient stone. With only a day left I hastily added some trees. Not good! But I turned it in anyway. A few days later the winners were announced. The art teachers had liked my church well enough to overlook the sorry trees and I was awarded a set of very good quality watercolors.

CHAPTER 7

BOMBING IN LONDON

In September the Blitz began and London was bombed every night. Every part of London was attacked, but the East End was almost destroyed as the docks were bombed with high explosives and set ablaze with incendiaries. Buckingham Palace was hit, so even the King and Queen were "bombed out", although they did, of course, have a few extra palaces to fall back on! Like me, the princesses had been evacuated, but they weren't living with strangers, and their "billet" was Windsor Castle.

My mother wrote frequently. There had been some bombing in our neighborhood, but no one we knew had been hit. One morning she had gone out to the back garden to feed our pet guinea pig, Mr. Nemo, and had found him dead. The cage was intact and there was no shrapnel nearby, but there had been many very loud explosions during the night. He had evidently died of shock or fright. Poor Mr. Nemo. Before the war I had shared my oranges with him. I was sad to think I wouldn't see him again.

Girls who had stayed in London after the summer holiday came back to Northampton after their homes were bombed. Sometimes their mothers came with them and they moved into small flats or rooms, because in London they had nowhere to live.

Even Northampton had an air raid. While the siren wailed and we hurriedly put on dressing gowns and slippers, a distant but solid thud sent us racing for the cellar steps where we huddled until the All Clear. The bomb had fallen two miles away in a field and no one was hurt. With its boot-making industry and agriculture, Northampton was not a target area, but planes often flew over on their way to somewhere else. Like most children, I had acute hearing and could soon distinguish between the sounds of English and German planes.

One night in mid-November I lay in bed, not yet asleep, hearing the odd, pulsing sound of enemy planes. There had been no air raid warning so I stayed in bed, but the planes kept coming, with no let-up in the sound. An hour went by and still the droning continued. Auntie Em came in, but she didn't know what it could mean. There must be hundreds of them. At last I fell asleep, with the ominous noise still in my ears. In the morning we knew that Coventry, many miles to the north, had been bombed all night, the city smashed and the ancient cathedral a charred ruin. Hundreds were dead, and survivors were digging huge graves for mass burials.

The war seemed closer all the time. Mr. Johnson was called up into the Air Force, and Uncle Fred joined the Home Guard, a group of elderly men whose weapons were mostly shovels and pitchforks. In spite of everyone's protests, he often was out all night "on maneuvers". Many of the men, like Uncle Fred, were veterans of the Great War of 1914 - 1918.

My brother and sister got homesick and went back to London. Many families were choosing to be together in spite of the air raids, and the government had begun to open some of the London schools. My school was still closed so I stayed in Northampton and prepared for another Christmas away from home.

Food rations were even tighter; the Christmas turkey was only a chicken, and the pudding was small. Presents from home were mostly money, since it was hard to shop during the air raids.

At last, my school reopened in London but with limited classes and teaching staff. Many of my friends and some of my favorite teachers went back. I felt cut off, missing all the excitement!! In February I went home.

CHAPTER 8

AT HOME IN THE BLITZ

My first evening in London was scary for me but the rest of the family seemed unperturbed. At seven o'clock the first siren sounded in the distance, followed by other sirens, closer to home. My mother declared, "Jerry's right on time!" but nobody went to the shelter. Weeks ago everyone had come to the conclusion they might survive in bed but would surely die of pneumonia in the cold damp shelter.

The noise began immediately. There were distant thuds, and not-so-distant explosions that shook the house, but my mother kept on knitting and my father continued reading the newspaper. My sister motioned me into the hall and upstairs to our parents' dark bedroom. We were forbidden to go near the windows but we did it anyway, peering between the blackout curtains. A plane that looked tiny, like one from my brother's toy plane collection, was silhouetted by crossed searchlights. Ack-Ack guns thundered and flares drifted down the sky. Another series of thuds and explosions, more Ack-Ack fire, and then everything was quiet. I went to bed, but lay awake until the All Clear sounded.

Next morning I went to school, and as I walked to the bus stop I looked around at the familiar yet changed neighborhood. Iron railings and gates that had fronted the houses were gone, salvaged to make munitions. Some windows were boarded up, and many were crisscrossed with tape to prevent shattering. A tiny building, almost hidden by sandbags, displayed the sign ARP WARDEN, and Archie, our former milkman, waved to me from the doorway. He was wearing a helmet - we called them tin hats.

Along the High Road, which was as noisy as ever, some shop windows displayed a few things for sale. There were lacy nightgowns and slips for women, leather shoes for men, hanks of knitting wool and a few bolts of cotton fabric. The green-grocer was arranging vegetables in front of his place, but the bicycle shop had no shiny *new* bikes and only three rather dilapidated secondhand ones. Other shop windows were boarded up, with tiny BUSINESS AS USUAL signs, but some of the shops were now only brick rubble. High up, in what had once been an upstairs flat, a bathtub still clung to a wall, and shreds of flowered wallpaper flapped against rain-soaked plaster.

The main entrance to the school was impressive with stone steps leading up to massive wooden doors, but one end of the building was sandbagged from ground to roof. I went to the office and was directed to a classroom where I greeted several old friends as I was given a desk. Lessons were often interrupted by air raid warnings, and we trooped into the gym which now did double duty as our air raid shelter. This was the sandbagged area I had observed earlier.

Otherwise, it was school as usual: French conjugations, German declensions, Science and Shakespeare, History and Mathematics, barely edible lunches of macaroni cheese and tapioca in the dining room, and Friday afternoons on the playing field. We were learning LaCrosse, after a fashion. Days began with hymns and prayers and admonishments against sliding down the banisters or, worse, sliding on the rare Australian hardwood floors, since they could not be replaced during wartime. The floors really were beautiful: dark red-brown laid in herringbone pattern and polished to a soft sheen, but they did make a good slide!

I settled into the routine: school, air raids, home for tea, more air raids, off to bed to wait for the All Clear. One night it didn't come. I was barely asleep when my bed began bouncing up and down, keeping time with the thunderous noise right outside my window. My mother came in; not to worry, it was only anti-aircraft fire. A very large gun traveled up and down the railway which was about a half mile from our house; the gun must be closer than usual. My bed bounced several more times, giant hailstones rattled on to the roof, and I went back to sleep. Next morning Michael added the shrapnel to his cigar box collection of jagged bits of bomb and shell fragments, and a piece of white silk braid from a landmine parachute.

I learned new vocabulary: thousand pounders; land mines; stick of bombs; oil bombs; incendiaries; and Molotov cocktails (bombs inside a bomb, like those Russian nested dolls we used to play with - or was that the Molotov breadbasket?).

My brother Ron, who was nineteen, regaled us with stories of helping the ARP wardens during raids. He had one particularly gruesome tale: a thousand pound bomb had fallen not far away and a woman was blown from her bed and impaled on the iron railings in front of the house. He had tried to pull her off! All that remained of the scene now was a flattened expanse of rubble.

My eldest brother, Denis, took his turn with other neighbors on fire watch duty. They learned to use stirrup pumps to douse the incendiaries that fell, but they seemed to like the camaraderie.

Sometimes on Saturdays I helped my mother with the shopping. If there was a queue at one of the shops we joined it even if we didn't know what it was for! There must be *some* reason people were standing in line! It might be a small cake that didn't taste quite like cake, or rayon stockings that didn't quite fit.

We could always get our basic rations, but sometimes there was only one egg per person for a whole month. We no longer could have eggs for breakfast, only for dinner. If we were lucky there might be a piece of bacon to go with it. My mother was adept at stretching the meat ration, and with a pound of beef she could make a gigantic pot of stew that fed us all for two days. Lots of dumplings and potatoes of course! Rabbits were not rationed and when the butcher had some it was worth a long wait to get one. It would make a wonderful pie.

As an island nation, the British had always had a bountiful supply of a wide variety of fish. There was finnan haddie, poached and buttered, and smoked kippers, as well as shrimp and mussels and other shellfish.

Now there were few men available to go out in the boats, and a great deal of danger for those who did venture out. The fish shops were closed most of the time, or they had only chips (French fries), but when the sign went up, FISH TODAY, people crowded in, waiting while the potatoes and battered fish sizzled in the big vats. No choice of plaice or halibut, but we felt lucky to get an extra meal.

The Easter holidays came. One morning I rode my bike past my school and stared at the shambles left by a landmine that had fallen during the night. Had it fallen during a school day all of us, students and teachers, would have died! A direct hit had destroyed our gymnasium / air raid shelter. Surprisingly, many of the front windows were intact, but the back of the building was heavily damaged and the entrance steps now led to a gaping hole where the huge doors had been. The assembly hall was open to the sky, its floor a mound of rubble from which protruded a thousand matchsticks of rare Australian hardwood!

The ARP men arrived and warned me away. Across the street the shopkeepers were sweeping up broken glass, but a sign on the sweet shop said OPEN FOR BUSINESS so I went in. Boxes of chocolate bars, a bit dusty but otherwise intact, were piled on the counter. Luckily, I had some pocket money - it was the first chocolate I had had in ages. A few days before, in that same shop, I had heard the usual "Sorry, no sweets today." Candy, like cosmetics, cigarettes, and other things in short supply, was always "under the counter" and reserved for friends or special customers. That day, with debris everywhere and the rain coming in, the shop owner was happy to sell to anyone!

The Easter holiday was extended until enough of the building could be declared safe. Rubble was cleared away, broken windows boarded up, and unsafe areas roped off. We crossed the street to the boys' school for gym classes, and since we no longer had a dining room we brought sandwiches from home. Sometimes they had strange fillings like SPAM or peanut butter. Lend-Lease had begun. Spam was quite tasty, and my sister loved peanut butter, but it took me a while to learn to like the sticky stuff.

My brother Ron joined the Air Force and was sent to Iceland. His address was Kaldadarnes, but he always wrote it "Kaldazell"! Even in summer it was bleak and windy, and the roof blew off the wash house the day after he arrived. "If this is summer," he wrote, "heaven help us when winter gets here!" But we were fascinated by his descriptions of wondrous geysers and nights lit by the Aurora Borealis.

CHAPTER 9

SUMMER RESPITE

There were hardly any raids that summer, and we basked in the warm days and the long, light evenings. We could swim in the park pool, play tennis, or ride bikes. Our northern latitude was an advantage now, and with clocks on double summer time it was light until almost midnight.

I went to visit my aunt and uncle and saw their new Morrison shelter. They had a beautiful back garden with roses and a lush green lawn, beds of colorful flowers, and a row of espaliered fruit trees hiding the vegetables and berries of the kitchen garden. Not wanting to spoil it by digging it up for an Anderson shelter, they had chosen the Morrison which was installed in the bedroom, with mattress and bedding inside. The top and bottom were heavy steel, with wire mesh panels on the sides. If the house collapsed they would be safe inside, but trapped until someone could dig them out. I don't think they were happy sleeping in their cage, and the next time I went to their house the mattress was on top of the shelter!

Propaganda was all around us, with posters and slogans in trains and buses and stretched across ruined walls: V FOR VICTORY; BRITAIN CAN TAKE IT; DON'T WASTE FOOD; CARELESS TALK COSTS LIVES; CARRY YOUR GAS MASK; IS YOUR JOURNEY REALLY NECESSARY? DIG FOR VICTORY!

Digging for Victory was easy for the English. Almost everyone loved to garden. A large section of our lovely green park was now vegetable plots, and our own back garden sprouted potatoes and green onions, with runner beans and tomatoes growing along the fence.

More food was rationed and even cornflakes and canned peaches required points. In June we were issued ration books for clothes and shoes. I grew out of everything twice a year and there were never enough coupons so I began the new term wearing a friend's outgrown uniform.

CHAPTER 10

WINTER AGAIN - BACK TO WAR

Dusk came earlier as another winter approached. Coal was now rationed and only one of the five or six fireplaces in a typical London house was likely to have a fire in the grate. Air raid sirens occasionally reminded us that we were now in our third year of war. I read about a family that had gone to their shelter one night. During a quiet spell, while the mother was in the house making tea, a direct hit on the Anderson shelter killed everyone in it. But the mother survived. So much for air raid shelters!

On December 7th the Japanese bombed Pearl Harbor and the United States was going to join us in the war. The first Americans appeared in London, seldom in the suburbs where I lived, but they crowded the theatres and restaurants of the West End. We were amused to see the Air Force officers wearing uniforms that didn't match, with dark jackets and pink trousers, but we thought they looked smart anyway!

My brother came home from Iceland, bringing skates, and introduced me to ice-skating at the Bayswater rink. I loved the quietness of it, compared to the roller rink, although I occasionally spent time drying out in the boiler room! But I was soon zipping around the ice, even backwards! Ron was accepted into Flight School and went off to the north for training.

In July there was much jubilation over the British victory at El Alamein, and the church bells rang in celebration.

Now I'm a teenager!

CHAPTER 11

WARTIME TEENAGERS

I joined a club for teenagers that had been started by one of the churches, with a different activity planned for each weeknight. On Wednesday we played table tennis or billiards, while a group of boys in a would-be band tried to play "Blues in the Night" - it was the only number they knew but they never got it quite right! Not many turned out for the Friday night discussions, and the Tuesday drama club was only a small group. But *everyone* came for the Thursday night dance! The orchestra was only a piano and one violin, but the girls put on their best dresses and curled their hair. And there were boys!

On Monday nights the Gilbert and Sullivan group met for rehearsals of The Mikado. Adults were allowed to join this group, but except for Nanki Poo and Yum Yum, who were waiting to be called up, almost everyone was under 18 or over 50. After weeks of practice we gave numerous performances at the church and were invited to perform in other areas of London. I was only in the chorus, but it was great fun, and I looked quite Japanese in my colorful kimono and obi, with tiny fans tucked into my black wig and my European skin and eyes hidden under Oriental makeup.

In the Autumn, the director at the Harrow Coliseum Theatre heard about our Gilbert and Sullivan group. He was struggling with the labor shortage and rehearsals were about to begin for the Christmas pantomime, so we were invited to audition for the chorus. I found myself in show business!

An English pantomime, a long-time Christmas tradition, has nothing at all to do with mime, but is a combination of music and dancing and comedy, arranged rather loosely around a fairy story. The principal boy, or Prince Charming, is always played by a woman, and the female "heavies" such as the ugly stepsisters in Cinderella, are always played by men! The Harrow pantomime that year was to be Sleeping Beauty. Like The Mikado, Sleeping Beauty had a cast that was mostly too young or too old, but makeup can do wonders and we looked pretty good. I loved singing and was taking lessons from a local Welsh music teacher, but I envied the high-kicking girls in the dance troupe, especially when they flew above the stage on invisible wires. One night they came looking for a replacement for one of the fairies who was sick, and I was chosen to put on the gauzy pink dress and waft my way across the dimly lit stage where the baby princess lay in the cradle. I was sure that the stage would be the life for me - some day I'd be a star!

I would have been happy to perform for free, but the pay was five shillings for each performance, six nights a week plus Saturday matinees. The show ran several weeks so this was more pocket money than I had ever had. I used some of it to buy my first pair of slacks. Some of the older generation were appalled at the sight of girls and women wearing trousers, but slacks were absolutely the "in" thing for teenagers. Mine were brown worsted with faint stripes. Another new fashion was the siren suit, a one-piece garment meant for wearing over pajamas during air raids, but now being worn any time of day. Even Mr. Churchill wore one. It was also chic to carry your gas mask in a fancy case - mine was maroon imitation leather.

After the pantomime closed I began going to the teen club again, usually meeting several of my friends and taking the bus. One evening it was very foggy, but four or five of us had found our way to the bus stop. At last the bus came, moving extremely slowly, the conductor walking along the curb, carrying a flaming torch to guide the driver. They were only going to the garage and there would be no more buses that night. This was not ordinary fog, even for London! The great city is at a low altitude, straddling the River Thames and not far from the sea. These geographical features were often the cause of very dense fog, and when the fog was combined with the smoke from the coal fires of eight million Londoners trying to keep warm the result was what we called a "pea souper". Now we had added the blackout and this was the blackest fog anyone could remember.

......But we were teenagers! No buses? We all walked up the road to the Underground station and got on the next train. Two stops later the train came to a halt but the doors remained closed. It seems the driver, unable to see the platform, had gone past it. The train started up again and at the next station we got off, went back one stop on the next train, and at last found ourselves out on the road, about a half-mile from the church. We couldn't see anything at all, but one of the boys had a flashlight and by holding it six inches from the ground we were able to follow the curb, holding on to each other and laughing hilariously, until we realized the curb had gone around a curve on to a different street! We backed up, got on the right road again, and at last found ourselves at the church. All the doors were locked! No one else was crazy enough to be out on such a night! There was nothing for it but to go home - on foot, of course!

My friends and I were learning to find our way around London on the Underground. Not underground at all where we lived, but several stops later the trains entered a tunnel and plunged into the darkness of the tube, the vast system of crisscrossing tracks beneath the heart of London, sometimes **hundreds** of feet beneath it. One day I rode into the West End with several friends to go shopping. We got off at Oxford Circus which is far below the surface, and took the long escalator up to the street.

We loved the big West End department stores, even when we didn't have enough money or coupons to buy anything. And the lunchrooms served up Lend-Lease eggs on toast, or waffles with ersatz chocolate sauce. Smaller shops displayed elegant clothes and shoes, antique jewelry, and sometimes things you would never find in the suburbs, such as the enormous ostrich egg I saw in one window! For three shillings you could have scrambled eggs for the whole family!

Out on Oxford Street and Regent Street we were fascinated by the assortment of uniformed people who crowded the sidewalk. We saw British soldiers, sailors and airmen in familiar khaki, navy and blue, and women in ATS, WAAFS and WRENS uniforms, or the jodhpurs and slouch hats of the Women's Land Army. Some uniformed men wore shoulder patches which read POLAND, NORWAY, DENMARK or CZECHOSLOVAKIA. There were Americans, Canadians and Australians, and French sailors with pompoms on their hats.

In the late afternoon we joined the after-work crowds who jammed the platform and crowded on to the train. Standing room only and you couldn't fall down even if you tried! At Baker Street we were startled by the order over the speakers to "All Change! All Change!" The crowd surged on to the platform and up the escalator to the street. Buses were waiting to take us past the next two stations to Finchley Road. An unexploded bomb was lodged just above the line at Swiss Cottage. It had fallen the night before, so we had ridden under it earlier in the day! That section of the line is near the surface so an explosion would be disastrous. Swiss Cottage was still there the next time I rode the train so they must have got the bomb out safely.

Each branch of the service had its own training corps, and many teenage boys (and some girls) were joining. They would be called up at eighteen and the training corps would get them into the branch of their choice. I'm not sure what the "training" involved, and I was too young to join, but on Saturday nights the groups often sponsored local dances and teenagers flocked to them.

Londoners loved films and the cinemas were full every night. Judy Garland and Mickey Rooney were great favorites, and everyone adored Deanna Durbin. We cried through "Mrs. Minniver", laughed through "Helzapoppin" and were amazed by "Gone With the Wind." Often a sign flashed on the screen AIR RAID IN PROGRESS but the film continued and we ignored the sign and the air raid.

Getting home afterwards was sometimes a challenge. Buses were on "skeleton" service, which I think had something to do with people who did not survive the long wait at the bus stops! When one did come along we could not see it until it got close because of the blue windows and very dim hooded headlights. We had to ask the conductor where it was going since there was no destination sign on the front. Sometimes, in an effort to keep our feet warm, we walked to the next stop, only to have a bus pass us between stops. We could only give up and walk all the way, hoping the fish and chip shop would be open so we could get hot chips to eat as we walked while the warm newspaper package kept our hands warm.

CHAPTER 12

ON THE HOME FRONT

Evenings at home were usually spent listening to the wireless. There were special stations now that catered to the American troops, and we could listen to Command Performance and Bob Hope and Jack Benny. In the early days of the war about the only comedy on the BBC was ITMA (It's That Man Again). Several times a day Tommy Handley and his cohorts, including Mrs. Bagwash and her daughter Nausea, Senor So-So, and Funf the spy, made fun of everyone and everything, especially the war. Tommy was the Mayor of Foaming-at-the-Mouth, or the Squire of the Manor of Much Fiddling, or Minister of Aggravation. It was hilarious, and a welcome relief from war news. Churchill was sometimes on, making us all feel like heroes, and if we tired of the impeccable diction of announcers like Frank Phillips and Alvar Liddell, we could always tune in Lord Haw Haw, our home-grown traitor now broadcasting from Germany. No one took him seriously, but he was always good for a laugh!

From the radio we learned the words to all the new songs: A NIGHTINGALE SANG IN BERKELEY SQUARE, WE'LL MEET AGAIN, SCATTERBRAIN, ROOM 504, YOU'D BE SO NICE TO COME HOME TO and MOONLIGHT BECOMES YOU. We went "Swingin' on a Star with Bing and rode the "Trolley" with Judy. Some of the lyrics were patriotic, like "There'll Always be an England" and others yearned for the end of the war, none better than "White Cliffs of Dover" sung by Vera Lynn.

One evening, as we sat listening by the fire, we were startled by a loud crash and found the front door wide open. The blast from a bomb had ripped the lock away from the door jamb, but the glass panels in the door were unbroken! Weird! It was the only damage our house sustained during the war, but it was easily repaired.

A young married woman who was expecting her first baby moved into the house next door. Her Air Force pilot husband was away, but a couple of weeks later he came home on leave, and we chatted across the back fence. He was very handsome in his lieutenant's uniform. A day or two later she went to the hospital and gave birth to twins. He went back to his base, took off on his first mission, and never came back. He was the only person I knew who died during the war, although one girl at school lost a little sister in an air raid. Now it seems rather amazing that my family and the families of my relatives and close friends all emerged intact from the war, but I didn't think about it then. We were young! We would live forever!

CHAPTER 13

LONDON NIGHTLIFE: BLACKED OUT BUT STILL THERE

The big West End theatres, as well as smaller suburban ones, enticed people with plays and musicals, opera and ballet, and there were Sunday concerts at the Albert Hall. Even the best seats were not very expensive, and for a couple of shillings my school friends and I could sit in the top balcony (we called it "up in the gods"). We saw Margot Fonteyn in "Swan Lake" and theatrical greats like Robert Donat and John Mills, and sometimes got our programs autographed at the stage door. Covent Garden Opera House had been turned into a dance hall, a mecca for the jitterbug crowd, but the rest of the theatres were playing to packed houses. At the beginning of the war most of them had been closed for a time, and only the Windmill Theatre could boast "We Never Closed!" It was on all their posters. When we left the theatre and headed for the Underground station we sometimes got a bonus sound-and-light show from the rocket guns in Hyde Park as the shells made red streaks across the sky.

Waiting for a train home we shared the platform with people sleeping in bunks lined up along the wall. They were all ages, elderly men and women and young children, some simply afraid to stay in their homes at night, others who no longer *had* homes.

There were plenty of restaurants in London. In the blackout they were almost invisible with blacked-out windows and double-curtained entries, but we managed to find them and they were always crowded. The government had set a price limit of five shillings for a meal and the chefs devised ingenious ways to make a profit as well as produce something that looked and tasted like food. Italian spaghetti and Chinese Chop Suey needed little or no meat, but other things were more of a mystery! One tucked-away place near Piccadilly always had steaks smothered in onions. No-one had that much beef, and it was rumored there was a small sign in the corner explaining it was horsemeat, but no-one went looking for it. And onions? Most people had to make do with leeks!

A new café opened with American-style food. I went there once and had Baked Ham with Raisin Sauce and Cole Slaw. It was quite good, by wartime standards, and there were quite a few American customers. Americans also liked the Trocadero which was an elegant place with white tablecloths, waiters in tuxedos, and an orchestra playing for dancing, but we always wondered where their "breast of pigeon" came from! Trafalgar Square was only a short distance away!

CHAPTER 14

D DAY

Spring came and the trees turned green under warming skies. Suddenly, the West End streets seemed eerily quiet, and we wondered where all the soldiers and sailors had gone. On the evening of June 6th I was at the cinema, watching the newsreel before the main film, when we heard the words "This is D-Day!" The film showed thousands of ships moving across the English Channel towards the coast of France. It was impressive and exciting.

CHAPTER 15

TRYING TO LIVE A NORMAL LIFE

People began looking ahead. One of our neighbors bought a secondhand television set, even though there had been no BBC telecasts since 1939, and only a few before that. They expected television to come back as soon as the war ended and they wanted to be ready with their tiny six inch screen. In the meantime the set had a radio and phonograph.

One week we got oranges, the first tropical fruit we'd seen in years, except on Carmen Miranda's head! Small children had never tasted them before, and had to be coaxed to eat them. Sweets were rationed now and we got twelve ounces a month. I always used my whole ration for Mars bars and they were gone in one day, but it was better than the under-the-counter days.

We were always looking for ways to cope with clothes rationing. It was illegal to buy or sell coupons, but they were easy to come by. Families who had more children than money were happy to accept hand-me-downs and turn coupons into cash. Since formal evening clothes were socially unacceptable during wartime, even for the King and Queen, men took their tuxedos out of mothballs and gave them to their wives who had them tailored into elegant suits. A piece of parachute silk made a lovely white blouse, and we were constantly knitting pullovers and cardigans. Scarce silk stockings that had "laddered" could be repaired at one of the numerous invisible mending shops where women sat in the windows taking advantage of the daylight. But stockings required coupons and many women put on leg makeup, or got by with last year's fading tan.

I was still growing and suddenly found my swimsuit too short. New swimsuits were absolutely unobtainable, even if one had the coupons. Since I loved swimming I had to find a solution. I decided to cut my suit in half - I'd always wanted one of those Betty Grable two-piecers anyway! My suit was made of elasticized fabric and I was able to fashion a halter top and snug-fitting trunks. I got a few whistles from the boys when I tried it out at the indoor pool, and after swimming a couple of lengths I got bolder and climbed on to the springboard. As I streaked down through the water I suddenly realized the bottom half of my suit was not staying put! Frantically, I reached down and pulled it back up, hoping I had made enough splash to hide my embarrassment. I did no more diving in *that* suit!

There were thousands of refugees living in London. They were in our schools and neighborhoods, working in the shops and offices. Some were German but we were confident that anyone who posed a risk was safely detained. Many, of course, were Jewish. Although these people were sharing our short supply of food, they also provided desperately needed workers. Our small island was accustomed to invasions by foreign people. For thousands of years they had come. Celts, Romans and Vikings, Saxons and Normans; French Huguenots fleeing religious persecution, and Irish fleeing the potato famine. Like their predecessors, most of these new refugees would stay.

Since my return to London I had written letters to the Johnsons in Northampton, and they invited me to come for a weekend. It was early evening when I boarded the train and the journey usually took about ninety minutes, but about halfway there the train pulled on to a siding and stopped. Delays happened often, and people waited patiently without knowing the reason. On this occasion we waited for more than two hours, and when we finally arrived in Northampton it was completely dark and the last bus had left.

During the time I lived in Northampton I had often walked home from town, but only in daylight, and it was a long way. There were several people at the bus stop, and I discovered that one man was going to the same area. He said he knew the way, and would be happy to walk with me. I had grown up with stories of Jack the Ripper, and I was quite frightened by the prospect of going anywhere with a strange man at night, but I was even more scared of trying to find my way alone in the dark, so we set out together.

It was a moonless night, completely black, and we could not see each other at all. We chatted as we walked along and I told him about my time as an evacuee in Northampton and what life was like now in London. He was in the Air Force, home on leave, and he and his wife lived a little further out than the Johnsons so he had to pass right by their house. As he had promised, he *did* know the way and we wished each other goodnight at the Johnsons' gate. They were still up, but surprised to see me since they thought I had missed the train. I was very hungry by then but we were soon sharing a supper of cold pork pie and home-made mustard pickles ladled from the big stone crock in the pantry. I have never tasted mustard pickles as wonderful as those. It was very good to see them all again - they were my second family.

Next morning Auntie (Mrs. Johnson) had a surprise. While cleaning they had removed the drawers from the chest where I had kept my things and there was my painting of the air raid shelter. It had slipped down into the inside of the chest.

**Growing up and out of my swimsuit!!
And no way to get a new one!!**

CHAPTER 16

BUZZ-BOMBS, ETC.

The war reclaimed our attention. We called them buzz-bombs, robot-planes and doodlebugs. Officially, they were V-1s, the first of Hitler's Vengeance Weapons. The small stubby-winged planes had no pilots, and they flew low across the sky, with a ferocious roar from the crude jet engines. Then, fuel spent and engines silent, they plunged downward and exploded. They came day and night, to all areas of London, but we got used to them! As long as we could hear the noise we were safe; only in the sudden silence did we feel a few moments of fear. One afternoon one of them was right over our roof. The house was shaking and the noise was deafening, and then the engine shut off. Panic! We dived under the table, but they usually glided down and that one hit a half-mile away. On another day we watched from the back garden as a V-1 with stuck rudder passed nearby, circled around, and headed back in our direction. Then the engine stopped and we watched it drop out of the sky. It exploded ten seconds later; the bomb had fallen two miles away.

And then the V-2s came. There was no comfort interval with these. The rockets streaked into the stratosphere and down on to the city, making no sound until they exploded. Of course, if we heard the explosion we knew we were safe, for the time being.

The buzz bombs and rockets continued through the winter, but at last, in the spring of 1945, they stopped. But there was another noise from the London skies now. British bombers at night and American bombers during the day, all on their way to the continent.

I spent a weekend with my grandparents at Worthing on the south coast. The small resort town had been right under the path of the V-1s heading for London, and they called it Buzz Bomb Alley. My grandparents had fled to my aunt's home in the Midlands, but now they were back, and we could walk on the beaches that for six years had been barricaded and mined in anticipation of the invasion.

CHAPTER 17

VICTORY IN SIGHT

In April we were sad when President Roosevelt died. He wasn't *our* president, but many people cried. Before long we were *not* sad that both Hitler and Mussolini were dead and the war in Europe was almost over. I wanted to be part of the all-night West End celebration. My parents didn't object. Perhaps they remembered the end of *their* war.

Early May was sunny and warm, and each day we wondered if this would be the day of surrender. One evening I went to a West End cinema with a young American pilot. About

10 o'clock we came out and found enormous crowds of people, laughing, singing, dancing and climbing lamp posts. The war was over in Europe! All but signing the documents anyway, and that was close enough for Londoners! I told my date I wasn't going home, so he decided to stay and celebrate too. It was still daylight, a lovely summer evening, and even as darkness settled over the city it stayed warm. We joined the revelers, surging through the streets, from Piccadilly Circus to Leicester Square, on to Trafalgar Square and along the Victoria Embankment. Midnight found us sitting on the base of the statue of Abraham Lincoln in Parliament Square, listening to Big Ben strike twelve. At dawn we waited in line for breakfast at Lyons Corner House, then walked through St. James Park to Buckingham Palace to see the Royal Family on the balcony, waving to the cheering throngs.

I went home at last and the American pilot went back to his base. I saw him once or twice after that, but he was soon sent back to the States. I wonder if he remembers V-E night!

Of course, the War wasn't over. My brother was still in the Air Force, the British Navy was in the Pacific Ocean, and young men and women were still being called up. Food was more drastically rationed than ever, and the small milk ration was skimmed so completely it looked blue! Even soap was rationed.

But Britain, the island, was no longer defined by bombs and blackouts. The lights were on again, and the church bells were ringing.

V-J Day came four months later, in September. After six full years, the war was over.

Wedding Photo

CHAPTER 18

EPILOGUE: TEENAGE G. I. BRIDE

I was eighteen years old and wanted to marry the American soldier I'd met the year before. He was from Oregon and one of our neighbors warned me I would be going to dangerous Wild West country! I assured her he lived in a city and the wild days were long gone. Paul had been sent to Germany for the occupation so ours had been mostly a "mail order" courtship, but my parents liked him and were agreeable to the marriage. For generations it had been a tradition among British families that at least one child would go off to live in the "colonies". Two of my mother's sisters and one of my father's brothers were in Australia, and my father had a sister in Canada. Most of my friends had aunts, uncles and cousins living overseas. So I was carrying on a tradition.

Although the war was over, rationing and shortages were worse than ever. I couldn't have a long white gown and there would not be a three-tiered cake or a sumptuous banquet. I used my clothing coupons for a suit, a white blouse and black suede shoes. There were enough coupons left for a rayon nightgown and some silk stockings. Practical!

As soon as Paul secured the necessary papers and got leave he came to London and we were married in the Registry Office with only my family and a few close friends present. Afterwards we had a simple luncheon at our house and then we took the night train to Cornwall. The weather was gloriously sunny but all too soon the honeymoon was over and Paul was back in Germany. Almost immediately he received orders to return to the United States and was soon out of the army. Within a few weeks I had my passport and travel papers and was ready to begin my journey.

During the war the ocean liners like the Queen Mary and Queen Elizabeth had been stripped of their pre-war luxury as they were converted to troop transports. Now the big ships had become bride transports. About 100,000 British women had married foreign soldiers and would start new lives in distant countries, most of them going to the United States. Some had already left. One of my friends had sailed in the spring and had written me letters describing life in Seattle.

The train from London was a "G I Brides Only" special. It took us to a former British Army barracks in South England which was to be our home for several days while we were "processed". Four of us shared a room that was clean and reasonably comfortable. Meals were served in the mess hall and our servers were Italian men who had been taken prisoners during the war. At least, that's what I was told, but why hadn't they gone back to Italy? The war had been over for almost a year.

Our days were regimented. We had medical checkups and we were vaccinated for smallpox, even though vaccinations had been mandatory in Britain for decades. I had been vaccinated as a baby and got an immune reaction. Our passports and other documents were checked, luggage was examined, and we were given information about naturalization laws. Three days later we were on a train, en route to Southampton.

I had never been out of England but the idea of going across the ocean held no terrors for me. I had always been a "water person". One of my earliest memories is of being pursued by my brother as I ran down the beach to the water's edge. I had been swimming since I was six years old, in rivers, lakes, ponds, indoor pools and outdoor pools, as well as the sea, although the beaches had been off-limits during the war. Now I was eager to experience life on an ocean liner. The train took us right to the dock and we got our first view of the "Bridgeport" which was to take us across the Atlantic.

"We're going across the ocean in that dinky little boat?" I was dismayed at the sight of the slightly over 300 foot vessel (tiny by Cunard standards).

After we were on board we learned something of the ship's history. It had belonged to the Germans during the first World War, then had been assigned to America as war reparations. During World War II it had been a hospital ship and was now a transport, bringing members of the American Women's Army Corps to Europe and returning with a load of GI Brides.

I was assigned to a "cabin" along with 63 other shipmates. There were three rows of double deck bunks, with several portholes along the outside wall. We were on the port side of the ship and there was an identical 64 person bunk room on the starboard side, with a bathroom between us. On the deck above us another 128 women were settling into identical facilities. The women with children were on upper decks in the few staterooms the ship provided.

A public address system was soon giving us instructions. Where and when to go for meals, and which decks were available to us. We must stay out of areas marked "Crew Only". Crew meant Navy personnel who were responsible for keeping the ship running. Our only contact was with the Army Transport Commander and Army personnel who served under him. There were a few office workers, the Chaplain, doctor, pharmacist, and an officer who was a sort of Activities Director - I've forgotten his exact title.

Captain Activities Director (I'll call him Captain P) announced over the P A that we were going to be on the ship for two weeks. *Two weeks*? I thought it took four or five days to cross the Atlantic. If we wanted to volunteer for some sort of activity to help pass the time we could report to him at the office the next morning. Young mothers needed babysitters, for one thing. I wasn't exactly up to changing diapers or dealing with crying toddlers but I decided I would show up anyway. Perhaps there was something else.

It had been late afternoon when we boarded the ship and we would not be sailing until the following morning. We turned in to our bunks as the sea air turned cool. One girl had the top bunk in the center of the room, right under the ventilator. She shivered all night and was dismayed at the prospect of spending the entire voyage under that ventilator. The rest of us slept well but we all felt sorry for the girl in the middle.

The next morning I went to the office. Captain P asked if I could type. I could. Would I like to be editor of the ship's newspaper? In school I had always loved composition and I'd had dreams of being a journalist, but before I got any grandiose ideas I was shown a copy of the daily paper. The "Porthole Peeper" was two sides of a mimeographed sheet! I would be given a desk and typewriter and my job would be to fill up two legal-size blue stencils every day. The Porthole Peeper logo had to be traced with a stylus and the news of the day, which Captain P would get over the ship's wireless, would be typed on the first page. I would be allowed to put what I liked in the rest of the space. I took the job.

Meanwhile, the ship had got under way. I went up on deck to watch as we headed down Southampton Water towards the Atlantic. The Queen Elizabeth was in dock and as we passed alongside her I was amazed at the size, especially the height. There was deck above deck, rows and rows of portholes and windows, and gigantic funnels above everything. I craned my neck to look up at this seagoing skyscraper and became even more aware of the size of our tiny ship.

We moved further from shore as we headed west and the Cornish coast was barely visible as we said farewell to England. We got a glimpse of Ireland (home of my great-grandparents) and then we were on the open ocean. The day was warm and sunny and there were no ripples on the surface of the sea, but the Atlantic moves constantly, rolling away to the horizon like restless dark green hills.

I soon had my sea legs, and found myself walking easily with a rhythmic rolling motion. Some of the girls promptly became sea-sick and retreated to their bunks. I had no such problems, so at lunchtime, eager to sample the ship's cuisine, I headed for the dining area.

Meals were served cafeteria style on stainless steel compartmented trays. After so many years of rationing we were amazed at the amount and variety of food. We sampled everything, including chicken for dinner and eggs for breakfast, but those immaculately shining steel trays gave everything the same disinfectant flavor! And I don't think the cooks had their training at the Cordon Bleu. Most of us settled for a breakfast of cornflakes that came in little boxes, and helped ourselves to apples and fresh cold homogenized milk that tasted wonderful after our watery wartime skimmed milk. At lunch and dinner we picked hopefully at what was served and always ate the Neapolitan ice cream. PX candy bars helped us survive.

I started my job at the Porthole Peeper. The news was always waiting on my desk. It was mostly yesterday's baseball scores, but sometimes there was a reminder that we had moved into a different time zone and should move our watches back an hour. I asked the other girls for contributions and was given small news items, poems, drawings, and other tidbits. I wrote some items myself and did a few drawings and always managed to fill the two stencils which I handed to the sergeant who worked in the office. He put them on the mimeograph machine and I was soon heading back to my shipmates with an armload of just-off-the-press copies.

One day I decided the guys needed a pin-up girl. I drew a Betty Grable style bathing beauty, traced it on to the stencil, and the paper went to press. Later that day Captain P informed me that the Transport Commander was very upset. He absolutely did not want anything sexual! That's why we had so many roped off areas with "Crew Only" and "Brides Only" signs. The deed was done but I tried to make amends. For the next day's issue I traced the same figure but replaced the two-piece bathing suit with a Victorian style dress, long sleeved, high-necked and ankle-length, with a glimpse of high-button shoes! On my way to distribute the latest issue I saw the Commander and Captain P walking ahead of me. I hurried to overtake them and handed each of them a copy as I passed. I heard the Commander guffaw, "What a sense of humor!" I didn't look back.

I found a second job playing music over the PA system during the afternoons. The record collection was not large but had most of the popular songs and some classics. I sometimes played requested favorites as I announced, "This is for Mary's birthday," or " .. for Joan and David's anniversary." Otherwise, I chose my own favorites, leaning towards classical music. Bing Crosby and Deanna Durbin were always popular.

So I kept busy, and I wondered why some of my shipmates spent most of their time in the cabin, although some did help in the nursery.

As much as I loved the water, the unchanging circle of ocean grew tiresome, and I longed for a sight of land. The weather continued sunny and very hot and even the nights were warm. Four tiny portholes in our cabin let in very little air during the day and at night a member of the crew came in to close and fasten them. Now the girl whose bunk was right below the ventilator was the only one who could sleep. She had been more than compensated for her one chilly night at Southampton. We tried to cool off by taking showers but the warm humid air in the windowless shower room made it impossible to get dry. One day I washed my hair and discovered, too late, that the fresh water in the showers had been turned off. My hair was caked with salt and stiff as a board. I was distraught but a few hours later the fresh water was back; another shower and shampoo and I was back to normal.

On our last full day at sea I put together a souvenir edition of the Porthole Peeper with a drawing of our ship which I copied from a photograph. Then I went up on deck. Captain P had told me there was a storm off the New Jersey coast and we were about to get into rough weather. The sky had changed from blue to gray, and the smooth blue-green swells had become dark and violent. I looked down into a foaming trough far below the deck railing, and the next moment it rose up to meet me. Crew members were hurrying to close portholes, even on the upper decks. I went down to the cabin where my shipmates were busy sorting and repacking their belongings. Our main luggage had gone into the hold at Southampton and we had been living out of suitcases which we stashed beneath the bottom bunks. I smoothed the wrinkles out of my clothes as best I could and chose the outfit I would wear when we went ashore.

The next morning I was up early but not early enough. I had hoped to be on deck for the first sight of land but I found we were already close to Long Island. The storm had passed and the sky was blue again. Houses along the shore gleamed white in the sunshine. The ship slowed and we watched the pilot come on board. Soon the tugboats began nudging us towards the dock. We had arrived at Staten Island.

It was only 9 am but already it was hot and humid with no hint of breeze. I went up on deck but there was nothing to see except the dockside and other ships moored nearby. A crane began unloading baggage from the hold. Trunks and suitcases, tumbled together in what appeared to be a gigantic rope hammock, were hoisted high into the air, swung over the side and lowered to the dock. Just beyond the dockside buildings I saw two young women pushing baby carriages and with several small children in tow. Both women were shabbily dressed. Our Staten Island "welcome" was gray and dismal. Where was the Statue of Liberty? Where were the skyscrapers? I went back to the cabin.

An announcement over the PA system: All brides whose destination was New York or who were being met by their husbands were to go ashore today, as soon as they could be cleared by the Customs and Immigration officials who were about to come on board.

The rest of us would have to stay on the ship for at least another day.

After two more days of stifling heat, unappetizing food and boredom, I said goodbye to new friends who were bound for Florida and New Hampshire, Minnesota and Mississippi, and just about every state in between. In mid-afternoon I was on a bus with others who were headed west. The train journey on the Baltimore and Ohio Line would take us twenty four hours. Our destination was Chicago.

Two Pullman cars had been reserved for our group. Chicago was the hub for train travel, as it would later become the hub for airline travel, and once we arrived there we would be transferred to many different train lines which would carry us to our ultimate destinations. It was already dinner time and I made my way to the dining car with several of the girls I had met on the ship. I don't remember what we had to eat but I do remember that it was far, far better than the shipboard food, and elegantly served on white-clad tables. By the time we returned to our car the porters were already making up the sleeping berths and women were trying to get babies and small children ready for bed. These young mothers had already been traveling for almost three weeks, struggling with paper diapers and feeding schedules. I didn't envy them.

We arrived in Chicago in the early evening of the next day. I was to take the Union Pacific train, along with five other girls, and we had a wait of several hours before we could board. By then it was quite late and the curtained Pullman berths were already made up. I was assigned to an upper berth and Eleanor, the only other girl going to Oregon, was in the same Pullman car. The other four girls were going to California and were in a different part of the train. I climbed into my berth.

The next morning Eleanor and I found our way to the women's washroom at the end of our car. There were no showers but there was plenty of hot water. We dressed behind the curtains of our sleeping berths and went to the dining car for breakfast. We found the same elegant décor and service as on the other train, and numerous menu offerings including bacon *and* eggs for breakfast!

I met the people who were in the berth under mine. They were teachers, husband and wife, on their way home to Seattle from Washington DC, and they had many questions about our wartime experiences. I shared their table at lunch and expressed my concern that English table etiquette was not the same as its American counterpart. I wanted to fit in and they gave me instructions on eating with my fork held in my right hand, using my knife only for cutting the meat and then placing it across the plate while switching the fork back to my right hand. It would be many years before I adopted my present "international" eating style - whatever works best for what's on my plate! I've long pondered the reasons behind this American / European difference. Was there a shortage of knives during the early Colonial days? Did people have to cut their meat and then pass the knife on to the next person at the table?

During the train journey between New York and Chicago I had been impressed by how familiar the landscape seemed. Towns were quite close together and there were many trees. Now, as we moved westward from Chicago, the scenery began to change. The farm country of Iowa and eastern Nebraska had a wide open feeling. Endless fields rolled away from the train as the waves of the endless ocean had rolled away from the ship in mid-Atlantic. The western Nebraska and eastern Wyoming landscape was stark and treeless, and even in our air-conditioned train we could feel the heat. I had looked forward to seeing the Rocky Mountains but we passed through at night and by morning we were in Idaho. Trees again! But not the oaks and elms that had shaded the Indiana farmhouses; these were evergreens, the tallest I had ever seen.

The four California-bound girls were no longer with us. Their section of the train had been disconnected and had become part of another train heading southwest.

In the late afternoon of our last day on the train it began to rain. One of the passengers remarked, "It's raining! We must be in Oregon!" I'd heard about Oregon's rain but hadn't yet learned that much of the eastern part of the state is classified as a desert and rain is rare, especially in summer, that, in fact, *most* of the state is dry in July and August.

The porter woke us early the last morning and I scrambled down from my berth and hurried to wash and dress before the train arrived in Portland. The train tracks through the Columbia Gorge run along the edge of the river, and I looked through the window, across the vast expanse of water to the tree-clad slopes of Washington State. The rain had ended and the river sparkled in the sunshine and reflected the blue of the sky.

I gathered my belongings and promised to write to Eleanor who was to take a southbound train to a different part of the state. The train slowed and pulled into the Portland station where Paul was waiting for me.

FOOD MEMORIES

Before food pyramids and cholesterol warnings there were only calories, and during the war there were never enough. We ate whatever we could get, including suet, lard and beef drippings. In 21st century America we want quick, easy and low-fat, so I have made adjustments to most recipes.

SAVORY DISHES

SHEPHERD'S PIE
2 cups cooked ground beef
½ cup chopped onion
1 ½ cups brown gravy
Salt and pepper to taste
2 cups mashed potatoes
Milk

   Mix beef, onion, gravy, salt and pepper in 2 qt baking dish. Add enough milk to potatoes so they will spread easily over meat mixture.
   Bake at 375° for 30 minutes. Serves 4.

CURRIED MINCE

1 lb ground beef	2 cups water
½ cup chopped onion	1 - 2 Tbsps curry powder
3 Tbsps flour	Salt

In large saucepan cook beef with onion until golden brown. Stir in flour. Add water and curry powder and cook on medium heat, stirring, until thick. Add salt to taste. Serve with mashed potatoes.

BEEFSTEAK PIE

3 Tbsps butter	1 tsp salt
2 lbs round steak, cubed	½ tsp pepper
1 onion, chopped	½ tsp basil
1 cup sliced mushrooms	½ chopped celery
¼ cup flour	½ cup chopped carrot
2 ½ cups water	Pastry top

Melt butter in large heavy saucepan or Dutch oven. Saute steak and onion until brown. Stir in flour. Add water, seasonings and vegetables. Stir over medium heat until mixture thickens. Lower heat, cover, and simmer until meat is tender (about 1 ½ hours). Pour into deep pie plate. Cover with pastry and cut several small slits. Bake at 425° for 20 minutes, or until crust is golden brown.

LITTLE MEAT PIES

Pastry
1 lb lean ground beef
½ cup chopped onion
1 tsp salt
¼ tsp pepper
¼ tsp sage
4 Tbsps flour
½ cup water

Prepare enough pastry for two crust pie but cut into four 6" circles and four 5" circles. Line four small pie pans with the 6" circles.

Brown beef with onion; stir in seasonings and flour; add water. Cook, stirring, until thickened. Cool slightly. Spoon mixture into pastry-lined pans, cover with pastry circles and crimp edges. Prick tops with a fork.

Bake at 425° for 20 minutes or until golden-brown.

ECONOMY BEEF STEW WITH DUMPLINGS

1 lb stewing beef, diced
1 onion, chopped
¼ cup flour
3 cups water
1 tsp salt
½ tsp pepper
½ cup chopped celery
4 large carrots, diced
1 turnip, diced
4 large potatoes, cut into chunks
Dumplings:
1 cup flour

3 tsps baking powder
¼ tsp salt
2 Tbsps oil
½ cup milk

   In a large kettle cook beef with onion over medium high heat until browned. Stir in ¼ cup flour. Add water, salt and pepper and cook, stirring, until thickened. Lower heat and simmer one hour, stirring occasionally. Add vegetables and continue cooking 20 minutes.
   Dumplings: Mix flour, baking powder, salt, add oil and milk and shape into 12 balls. Drop into boiling stew, cover and cook 20 minutes.

RISSOLES

6 ozs cooked roast beef
½ onion, chopped
1 ½ cups mashed potatoes
½ tsp salt
Dash pepper
1 egg, beaten
Flour
1 - 2 Tbsps oil

   Grind meat and mix well with onion, potato, salt, pepper and egg. Shape into 8 flat round cakes and coat with flour. Heat small amount of oil in large skillet and cook rissoles until brown on both sides.

CORNISH PASTIES

½ lb lean ground beef
1 onion, chopped
1 turnip, grated
1 Tbsps flour
2 Tbsps chopped parsley
¾ tsp salt
Dash pepper
8 6" pastry circles

   Cook beef with onion and turnip until vegetables are tender and meat is browned. Add flour, parsley, salt and pepper; mix well. Cool. Divide mixture between pastry circles and fold in half. Seal edges and prick tops.
   Bake at 425° for 15 - 20 minutes, until crisp and golden-brown.

RABBIT PIE

2 - 3 lbs rabbit pieces
2 ½ cups water
1 tsp salt
¼ tsp pepper
½ bay leaf
4 Tbsps butter
½ cup chopped onion
4 Tbsps flour
9" pie crust

Place rabbit, water, salt, pepper and bay leaf in saucepan; simmer, covered, 1 hour. Remove rabbit pieces, reserving liquid. Separate meat from bones in as large pieces as possible and place in 9" pie plate.

Melt butter and cook onion until tender; stir in flour. Add cooking liquid, discarding bay leaf. Cook over medium heat, stirring constantly, until thickened. Pour over rabbit, cover with pastry crust and bake in 425° oven 20 minutes or until golden-brown.

TOAD IN THE HOLE

¾ lb link sausages
1 cup flour
½ tsp baking powder
½ tsp salt
2 eggs, beaten
1 cup milk
Brown sauce or gravy

Cook sausages slowly until well done, drain well and arrange in greased 8" square baking pan. Combine flour, baking powder and salt; add eggs and milk and beat well. Pour over sausages.

Bake at 450° 30 minutes or until golden brown and puffy. Serve with sauce or gravy.

MULLIGATAWNY

6 Tbsps butter or margarine

1 ½ cups chopped onion
1 apple, peeled, diced
¼ cup flour
6 cups chicken broth
½ cup coconut
2 Tbsps curry powder
2 cups diced cooked chicken
1 cup cooked rice

  Melt butter; cook onion and apple until tender; stir in flour. Add chicken broth, coconut and curry powder; cook over medium heat, stirring, until thickened. Add chicken and rice and cook until hot.

LANCASHIRE HOT POT

1 lb shoulder lamb chops, boned
1 onion, sliced
3 potatoes, peeled, sliced
2 Tbsps flour
1 cup water
2 bouillon cubes

  Cut chops into four pieces; brown in skillet. Place in greased baking dish. Top with onions and potatoes. Mix flour with pan drippings, add water and bouillon cube, cook until thick. Pour over potatoes. Cover and bake at 350° for 1 hour. Uncover and bake at 400° for 15 minutes.

FISH PIE

2 Tbsps margarine
2 Tbsps flour
1 cup milk
½ tsp salt
Dash pepper
1 cup cooked fish
1 Tbsps chopped parsley
2 cups mashed potatoes

   Melt margarine, stir in flour, add milk, salt and pepper and cook, stirring, until thick. Break fish into chunks and add to sauce with parsley. Turn into baking dish and spread potatoes over the top. Bake at 375° for 30 minutes.

FISH CAKES

2 cups cooked boneless fish
2 cups mashed potatoes
1 egg
½ tsp salt
¼ tsp pepper
Flour
3 Tbsps oil or shortening

   Mash fish with potatoes, egg, salt and pepper. Shape into eight patties, ½" thick, and coat with flour. Fry in hot oil or shortening until browned on both sides.

SALMON PASTE

1 can (1 lb) salmon, drained
4 ozs cream cheese
1 tsp lemon juice
Dash cayenne or pepper

Combine all ingredients in food processor or blender. Mix until well blended and very smooth. Turn into a glass serving dish, cover, and chill. Serve in sandwiches.

BEAN CHEESE

1 cup cheese sauce
2 cans white beans, drained
Shredded cheese

Combine sauce and beans, turn into baking dish and sprinkle shredded cheese over the top.
Bake at 350° 30 minutes.

WELSH RABBIT

6 ozs grated Cheddar cheese
2 Tbsps butter
3 Tbsps milk
½ tsp dry mustard
Dash cayenne
4 slices toast

Mix cheese with butter, milk and seasonings. Spread over toast and broil until bubbly and golden-brown.

PEAS PUDDING

1 cup yellow split peas
2 cups beef broth
½ cup chopped onion
1 tsp salt
1/8 tsp pepper

Soak peas overnight in cold water; drain. Combine all ingredients in saucepan, bring to boil, simmer until soft and thick, stirring frequently and adding water as necessary.

COLCANNON

2 cups water
1 tsp salt
Dash cayenne
Dash nutmeg
2 cups shredded cabbage
2 cups potato flakes
2 Tbsps butter
2 green onions, chopped

Combine water, seasonings and cabbage in 3 quart saucepan. Bring to boil, simmer 5 minutes. Stir in potato flakes, butter and green onion. Turn into 1 quart baking dish.
Bake at 325° for 30 minutes.

ROASTED POTATOES

3 medium potatoes
Oil
Salt and pepper

Peel potatoes and dry with paper towels. Cut into quarters, sprinkle with salt and pepper and place around roast meat for final hour of cooking, turning to coat with meat drippings. If there is very little fat, brush potatoes with oil before cooking.

YORKSHIRE PUDDING

1 egg
1 cup milk
1 cup flour
¼ tsp salt
¾ tsp baking powder
Brown gravy

Beat egg and milk together. Add flour, salt and baking powder; beat well. Let stand for 20 minutes. Beat again. Pour into greased 8" square baking pan. Bake at 450° for 35 minutes. Serve immediately with Gravy.

STEAK SAUCE

½ cup ketchup
2 Tbsps Worcestershire sauce

Mix well. Serve with steak or cold meat.

DESSERTS

COTTAGE PUDDING WITH JAM SAUCE

1/3 cup butter or margarine
¼ cup sugar
1 egg
1 ¾ cups flour
Dash salt
1 tsp baking powder
1/3 cup milk
1 cup jam, any flavor
¼ cup water

    Cream butter with sugar; beat in egg. Mix flour, salt, baking powder and add to egg mixture, alternately with milk. Turn into greased 8" square pan and bake at 375° for 35 minutes or until done.
    Mix jam and water in small saucepan; bring to boil, stirring. Pour over warm pudding.

EGGLESS BOILED CAKE

1 cup raisins
1/3 cup sugar
1/3 cup butter or margarine
1 cup water
1 ¾ cups flour
½ tsp cinnamon
¾ tsp baking soda

Combine raisins, sugar, butter and water in saucepan. Bring to boil and simmer 3 minutes. Cool completely. Mix flour, cinnamon and baking soda together. Stir in the raisin mixture and turn into greased 8" square baking pan. Bake at 350° for 30 minutes.

QUEEN OF PUDDINGS

3 egg yolks
¼ cup sugar
2 cups milk
½ tsp vanilla
2 Tbsps melted butter
2 cups soft bread crumbs
1/3 cup jam
3 egg whites
¼ cup sugar

Mix egg yolks with sugar; stir in milk, vanilla and melted butter. Add breadcrumbs, mix well and turn into buttered 6 cup casserole. Bake at 350° for 50 minutes, or until set. Spread jam over top of pudding.
Beat egg whites to soft peak stage. Beat in sugar one tablespoon at a time. Spread over pudding.
Bake 15 minutes to brown meringue.

BANBURY CAKES

1 cup dried currants
½ cup candied peel

1/3 cup sugar
2 Tbsps flour
¼ tsp cloves
¼ tsp cinnamon
1 egg, beaten
2 Tbsps oil
18 4" pie-crust squares
Sugar

   Mix fruit, sugar, flour, spices. Add egg and oil and mix well. Divide between pastry squares. Bring corners up over filling, overlapping. Turn over and flatten with palm of hand. Place on cookie sheet and sprinkle with sugar.
   Bake at 425° 20 minutes or until lightly browned.

VICTORIA SANDWICH CAKE

1 pkg white cake mix
2 Tbsps jam
Powdered sugar

   Prepare cake as package directions using two 8" round cake pans. Remove from pans and cool.
   Place one layer on a plate, spread with jam, top with second layer and sprinkle with powdered sugar.

GOLDEN FRUIT CAKE

1 ¼ cups chopped candied fruit
1 cup raisins

¾ cup chopped nuts
¼ cup cream sherry
¼ tsp almond extract
½ cup butter
¾ cup sugar
3 eggs
1 2/3 cups flour
½ tsp salt
¾ tsp baking powder
½ tsp mace or nutmeg

Combine fruits, nuts, sherry, almond extract. Cream butter and sugar, beat in eggs. Mix flour, salt, baking powder, spice and add to creamed mixture. Fold in fruit and turn into greased, floured 9" x 5" x 3" loaf pan.
Bake at 300° for 2 hours or until done.

BUTTERFLY CAKES

1 pkg white cake mix
Sweetened whipped cream

Prepare cake according to directions for cupcakes. Remove from cupcake pan and allow to cool. Slice off the top of each cupcake and cut into two to make wings. Spread whipped cream on each cake and add the wings.

MADELEINES

1 pkg white cake mix

Apricot jam
Coconut
Candied cherries

   Prepare cake mix according to package directions for cupcakes. Remove from pans and turn upside down. When cool spread jam over the top and sides and sprinkle with fine coconut. Top each with a cherry.
   (These will not be true Madeleine shape)

ROCK CAKES

2 cups biscuit mix
½ cup sugar
¼ tsp cinnamon
¼ tsp nutmeg
¼ tsp ginger
½ cup raisins
1/3 cup chopped candied peel
½ cup milk
1 egg
2 Tbsps oil or melted butter

   Combine biscuit mix, sugar, spices and fruit. Mix milk with egg and oil and stir into dry ingredients. Spoon on to greased baking sheet to form 12 mounds.
   Bake at 400° for 15 minutes

MINCE PIES

1 ½ cups prepared mincemeat
Pastry
Sugar

Roll out pastry and cut into twelve 3" circles and twelve 2" circles. Press the larger circles into a 12 cup muffin pan. Spoon 2 tablespoons mincemeat into each cup and place smaller pastry circles on top. Sprinkle with sugar.
Bake at 425° for 20 minutes or until golden brown.

LIGHT MINCEMEAT

2 apples, peeled, chopped
1 cup chopped candied fruit
2 cups raisins
½ cup brown sugar
1 tsp ginger
1 tsp cinnamon
1 tsp nutmeg
¼ cup orange juice
¼ cup brandy
2 Tbsps butter or margarine

Combine in 3 quart saucepan. Bring to boil, stirring, lower heat and continue cooking, stirring frequently, until apple is tender and mixture is thick (about 30 minutes). Store in refrigerator.

LIGHT CHRISTMAS PUDDING

1 cup raisins
1 cup candied fruit
1/3 cup oil
¾ cup brandy or orange juice
¾ cup brown sugar
2 eggs, beaten
1 ½ cups flour
3 tsps baking powder
½ tsp salt
1 tsp cinnamon
1 tsp ginger

Combine fruit, oil, brandy, brown sugar and eggs. Mix flour, baking powder, salt and spices. Add to fruit mixture and mix well. Turn into greased heatproof bowl. Cover with foil. Steam 3 hours. Serve hot.

MILK JELLY

1 pkg flavored gelatin
1 cup boiling water
1 cup evaporated milk

Combine gelatin with boiling water, stir until dissolved. Cool 20 minutes. Stir in milk. Chill until set.

BLANCMANGE

4 Tbsps cornstarch
3 Tbsps sugar
2 ½ cups milk
1 tsp vanilla or almond flavor
Few drops red food coloring

   Combine cornstarch and sugar in heavy saucepan with enough milk to make a smooth paste. Stir in remaining milk. Cook over low heat, stirring constantly, until thickened. Add vanilla or almond and food coloring. Pour into serving dish and chill until firm.

TRIFLE

8 slices sponge cake
¼ cup raspberry jam
1 cup fruit cocktail, drained
¼ cup cream sherry
1 pkg vanilla pudding (not instant)
2 ¼ cups milk
1 cup whipping cream
2 Tbsps sugar
Maraschino cherries

   Spread cake with jam. Place half in serving dish, drizzle with sherry, top with fruit. Add remaining cake and sherry. Cook pudding as package directs. Pour over. Cool. Whip cream with sugar, spread over Decorate with cherries.

JELLIED TRIFLE

6 slices sponge cake
1 large banana, sliced
1 pkg raspberry gelatin
1 cup whipping cream

   Cut cake into bars and arrange in glass serving dish with banana. Prepare gelatin as package directs and pour over cake and fruit. Chill until set. Whip cream with a little sugar and spread over the top.

RHUBARB AND APPLE TART

2 cups rhubarb chunks
2 cups sliced apples
¾ cup sugar
4 Tbsps flour
9" unbaked pie shell
12 narrow strips pastry

   Mix fruit with sugar and flour. Turn into pie shell. Lay pastry strips on top, lattice-fashion.
   Bake at 450° for 10 minutes. Lower heat to 350°. Bake 35 minutes.

BAKEWELL TART

9" unbaked pie shell
½ cup raspberry jam
¼ cup butter

2/3 cup sugar
2 eggs
½ cup ground almonds
½ cup fine breadcrumbs
2 Tbsps evaporated milk
¾ tsp almond extract

Spread jam in pie shell. Cream butter and sugar; beat in eggs. Add remaining ingredients and spoon over jam.
Bake at 450° for 10 minutes. Lower heat to 350°. Bake 20 minutes or until set.

STEWED FRESH FRUIT

2 lbs fresh fruit, any kind or combination
½ cup sugar
½ cup water

Wash fruit, remove peel, cores, pits, as needed. Place in saucepan with sugar and water. Bring to boil; simmer, covered, 15 minutes. Serve warm or cold with cream.

FRUIT FOOL

2 cups pureed or mashed fruit, any kind
1 cup whipped cream

Swirl together and spoon into dishes.

OLD-FASHIONED CHRISTMAS PUDDING

1 cup raisins
1 cup golden raisins
1 cup dried currants
1 cup candied peel
2 Tbsps orange juice
¼ cup brandy
1 cup flour
1 cup fine breadcrumbs
½ tsp cinnamon
¼ tsp nutmeg
¼ tsp ginger
1 cup sugar
1 cup shredded suet
1/3 cup chopped nuts
3 eggs, beaten
6 Tbsps milk

    Combine fruit with orange juice and brandy; mix well. In separate bowl mix flour, breadcrumbs, spices, sugar, suet and nuts. Combine the two mixtures with eggs and milk and mix thoroughly. Turn into greased heatproof bowl. Cover with waxed paper and several layers of cheesecloth. Tie string around to hold covering in place.
    Place pudding on a folded dishtowel in the bottom of a large kettle. Add water to reach halfway up the bowl. Cover kettle. Bring to boil and reduce heat so water is boiling gently. Cook for 6 hours, adding more boiling water from time to time. Remove pudding, cool, and cover with clean dry cloth. Store in refrigerator.

Before serving, boil the pudding for one hour. Serve hot.